STEP-BY-STEP

COLLAGE

JIM ROBINS
AND PHILIP STEELE

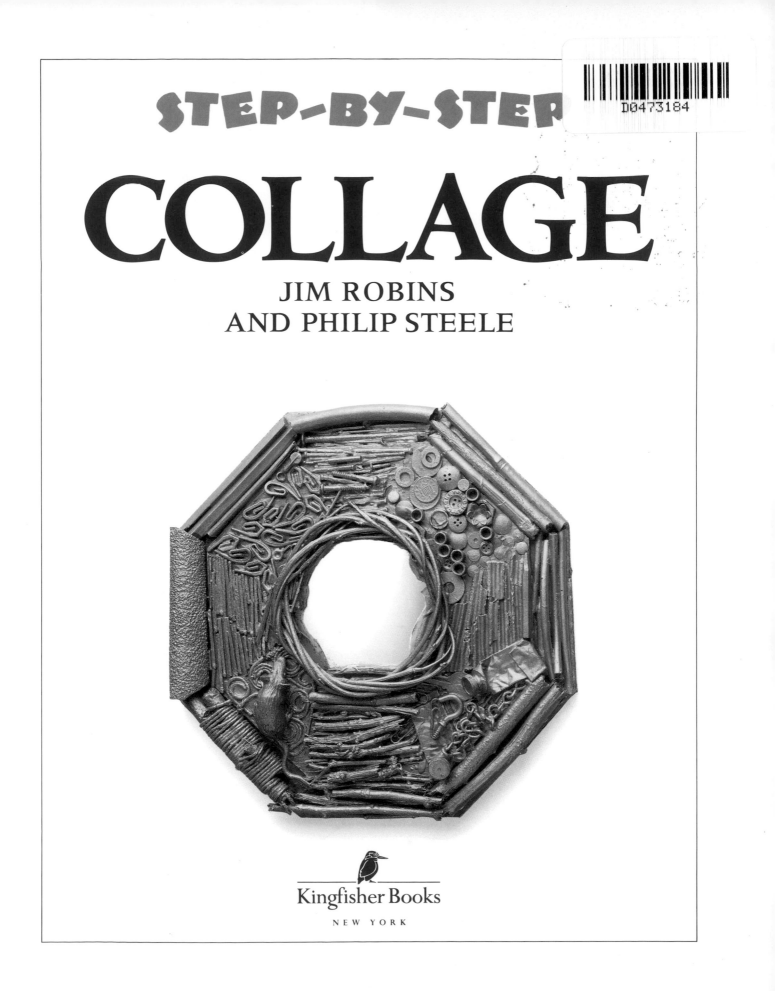

Kingfisher Books

NEW YORK

KINGFISHER
Larousse Kingfisher Chambers Inc.
95 Madison Avenue
New York, New York 10016

First American edition 1993
10 9 8 7 6 5 4 3 2 1 (lib. bdg.)
10 9 8 7 6 5 4 3 2   (pbk.)

Library of Congress Cataloging-
in-Publication-Data
Robins, Jim
   Collage/Jim Robins.
     p. cm. — (Step-by-Step)
   Summary: An introduction to
basic collage techniques, with
instructions for making various
kinds of collages out of paper
fabric, and other materials.
   1. Collage — Juvenile literature.
[1. Collage. 2. Handicraft.]
I. Title. II. Series: Step-by-Step
(Kingfisher Books)
TT910,S74 1993
702'.8'12 dc20 92-42678 CIP AC

ISBN 1-85697-921-0 (lib. bdg.)
ISBN 1-85697-920-2 (pbk.)

Edited by Deri Robins
Designed by Ben White
Illustrations by Jim Robins
Collages by Jim Robins pp 6-15,
18-21, 24, 28-39; Deri Robins
pp 22, 40; Philip Steele pp 17, 40.
Photographed by Rolf Cornell
Cover design by Terry Woodley

Printed in Hong Kong

CONTENTS

WHAT YOU NEED

Collages are pictures made by pasting down scraps of paper and other odds and ends. You will need scissors, glue, paper, and cardboard, and all the bits of junk you can lay your hands on.

Paper

Paper and cardboard are ideal for making collages. Try to build up a collection that includes some of the following: newspaper, magazines, tissue and crêpe paper, wallpaper, construction paper, wrapping paper, candy wrappers, tinfoil, sandpaper, junk mail, envelopes, postcards, tracing paper, smooth and ridged cardboard.

Add texture to paper by scrunching or folding it, or try wrapping it around a pencil to make curls. Or add patterns, by laying the paper over a raised surface and rubbing with a spoon.

Twigs and leaves

Fabric

Stapler

Hole punch

Fabric

Collages made from fabric are fascinating to touch as well as to look at. Collect scraps of cotton, wool, silk, leather, burlap, lace, and net, as well as ribbons and sequins. Fur fabric is especially fun to work with and can be bought quite cheaply in small quantities.

Bits and Pieces

Start a junk box, and save the following: egg cartons, string, straws, stamps, buttons, corks, beads, small toys, Styrofoam, bubblewrap, screws, washers, nails, nuts and bolts, bottle tops, leaves, shells, twigs, and dried pasta.

Tools of the Trade

In addition to scissors, you may need to use an art knife — these are sharp, so ask an adult to help.

Use safe, simple glues, such as white glue or glue sticks. Tape and a stapler are also useful.

Although collage is about gluing, you can add extra color with paint and glitter.

Finally, you will also need a ruler and pencils.

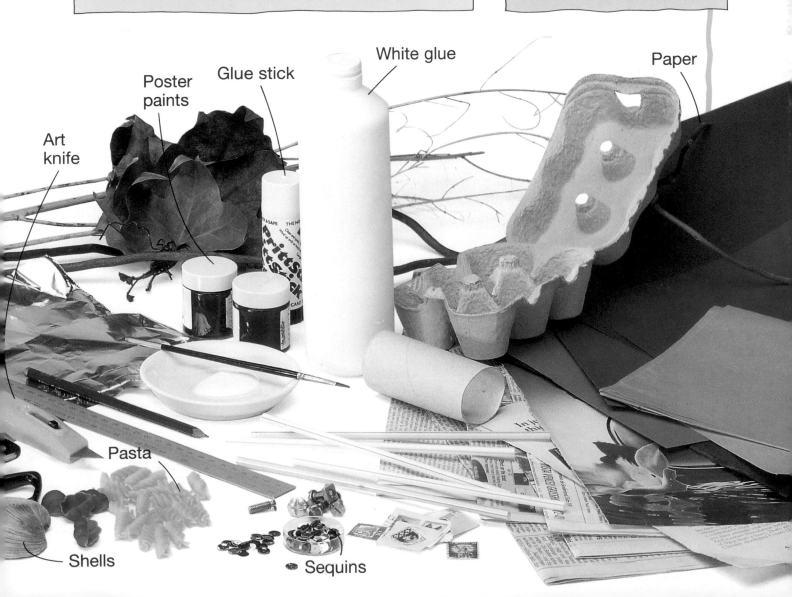

Poster paints

Glue stick

White glue

Paper

Art knife

Pasta

Shells

Sequins

PAPER PATTERNS

Paper is cheap, colorful, and very easy to cut and paste — which makes it perfect for collage. Save old magazines and newspapers, and look out for other types of paper and cardboard (see page 4).

Before you start to make pictures from paper, try arranging scraps in abstract patterns as shown here. Making patterns will help you to learn about color, shading, and texture — this will be helpful not only when making collages from paper, but also when you are using fabric and other bits and pieces.

Try combining cut and torn shapes in your pattern using black and white for bold contrast.

Cut dark-colored paper into shapes with scissors or an art knife. Glue them in a pattern onto a sheet of white paper.

In contrast to the clean, sharp lines of the cut paper, a similar pattern made from torn paper has a much softer feel.

For a more subtle contrast, try using the many different *tones* (or shades) of gray that lie between black and white.

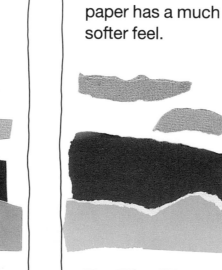

Experiment with color. Try soft pastel shades (below), or bright, cheerful colors. Which ones clash? Which ones work well together?

Red, orange, and yellow are warm colors. They can appear even warmer when a cool color is placed next to them, as here.

Blue, green, and purple are cool colors. While warm colors appear to come toward you, cool colors often seem to move away.

Try overlapping pieces of tissue paper to make new colors, or to make the same color richer.

Look for patterns in magazines, wallpaper, and wrapping paper. Cut them out, and use them in collage.

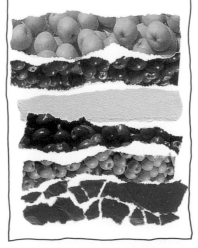

Add texture to your collages, mixing some of the many different types of paper. Add scraps of material and other finds.

CUT PAPER

Choose strong, bold-colored paper, and cut it into simple shapes to make striking collages. The one shown here is based on collages by the French artist Henri Matisse — try looking through art books in the library for more ideas.

1 Sketch your ideas for a collage, using some colored pencils or crayons.

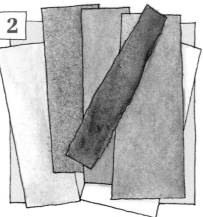

2 Collect paper for the collage. Check that the colors you choose go well together.

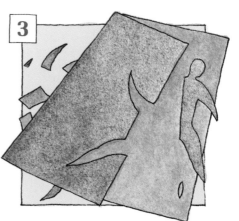

3 Cut the paper into shapes that match those in your drawing. Do the background first.

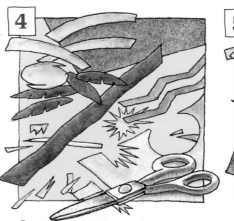

4 Cut out all the other shapes. Arrange the shapes on top of the background.

5 Move the shapes around until you like the way they look together. Glue them in place.

TORN PAPER

Pictures made from torn paper have a softer look than those made from cut paper. Tearing produces shapes with a feathery edge — if the paper is colored on one side and white on the back, you will also get a white line around part of the shape.

1

Sketch an outline for your collage, and gather your pieces of paper together.

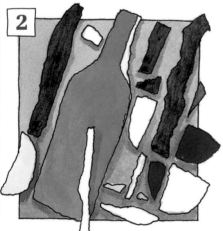

2

Tear the paper into shapes and glue them in place. Overlap with smaller pieces to add details and highlights.

Make a Mosaic

In ancient Rome, buildings were often decorated with mosaics — pictures made from tiny pieces of glass or stone set into plaster. Try making a mosaic from tiny squares of torn paper, as here.

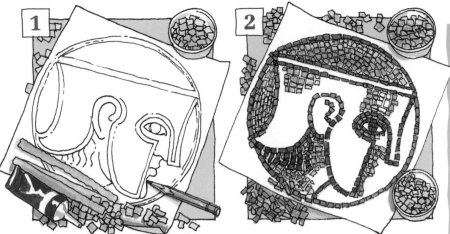

SCRAP PICTURES

Old magazines are ideal for collage. The paper is glossy, brightly colored, and full of patterns and letters which add interest to your finished picture. The magnificent crowing rooster shown below was made from a mixture of torn and cut paper.

1

Make some sketches for your collage on scrap paper, using colored pencils. Copy the outline on a piece of cardboard, and use it as a base for the collage.

2

Collect a pile of old magazines. Look for large areas of color, and tear them out. It doesn't matter if the pages have writing or pictures on them.

3

Tear or cut the pages into shapes for the collage. To make the rooster's tail feathers, press a round lid on the paper and tear around the curve.

4

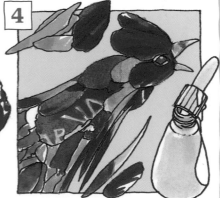

Arrange the pieces on the cardboard. Try to contrast bright, rich colors with darker areas. Overlap pieces of paper as shown, and glue in place.

WORDS AND PICTURES

Most newspapers are printed in black type on white paper. However, because the size and thickness of the type varies enormously, some areas look very dark while others are light. Try using this variety of *tone* to make pictures.

1

Find a picture with lots of contrasting tones, (one which contains light, dark, and medium shades). Draw the outlines on cardboard.

2

Look through some old newspapers, and tear out pages that have plenty of contrasting light, medium, and dark areas of print.

3

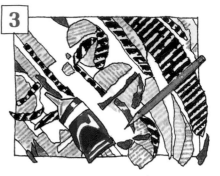

Cut or tear the paper into shapes that match the light and dark areas in your picture. Arrange them in position, and glue them down.

4

You can finish your picture by adding words — try making these by tearing or cutting letters from the paper.

You can also make words by cutting or tearing out the letters themselves from headlines or from other areas of large type.

Combine the letters with pictures cut from newspapers, photocopies, and magazines — or with drawings you have made yourself.

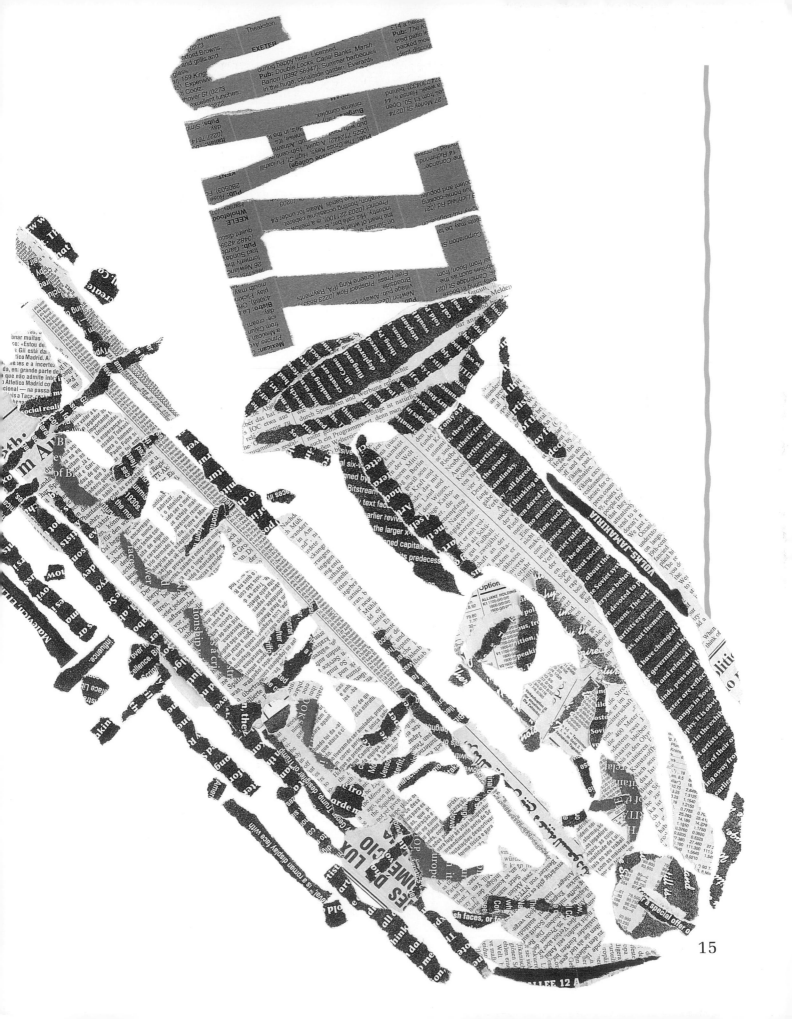

15

STICK-ONS

Some of the best material for collage is thrown away every day. Save used stamps, stickers, labels from food cans and bottles, seed packets, candy and cookie wrappers, sachets of salt and sugar; and glue them down to make pictures.

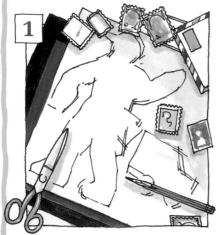

1 Draw a mail van and its driver on white cardboard. Draw slightly smaller ones on black paper, and glue on top.

2 Glue the van and driver to colored cardboard or paper. Glue used stamps to the picture, as shown opposite.

3 Use old envelopes as well — postmarks make good wheels and faces. Add features cut from plain black paper.

Cut the labels from cans of fruit, or pictures from color magazines. Use them to make a collage of a bowl of fruit.

Save candy wrappers, and glue them to cardboard to make a picture of a giant candy!

SILHOUETTES

Simple black shapes look dramatic against a light background, or hung up against a window. Draw your design on thin black cardboard or construction paper, and cut out the background with scissors or an art knife. For a stained-glass effect, glue colored tissue paper to the back of the cardboard.

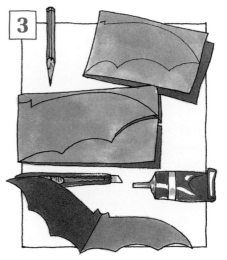

1 Draw the window frame, witch, and castle on a large sheet of black construction paper. Cut out the background.

2 Tape wide strips of tissue paper to the back of the frame. Cut out a moon for the light to shine through.

3 Fold different-sized strips of black paper in half to make bats. Cut them out, and glue to the window.

Try some more designs — how about a prowling panther in a cage? Stained-glass silhouettes are also popular at Christmas — they often show church windows, but you could try making a snowman, a reindeer, or a Santa Claus.

FUN FABRIC

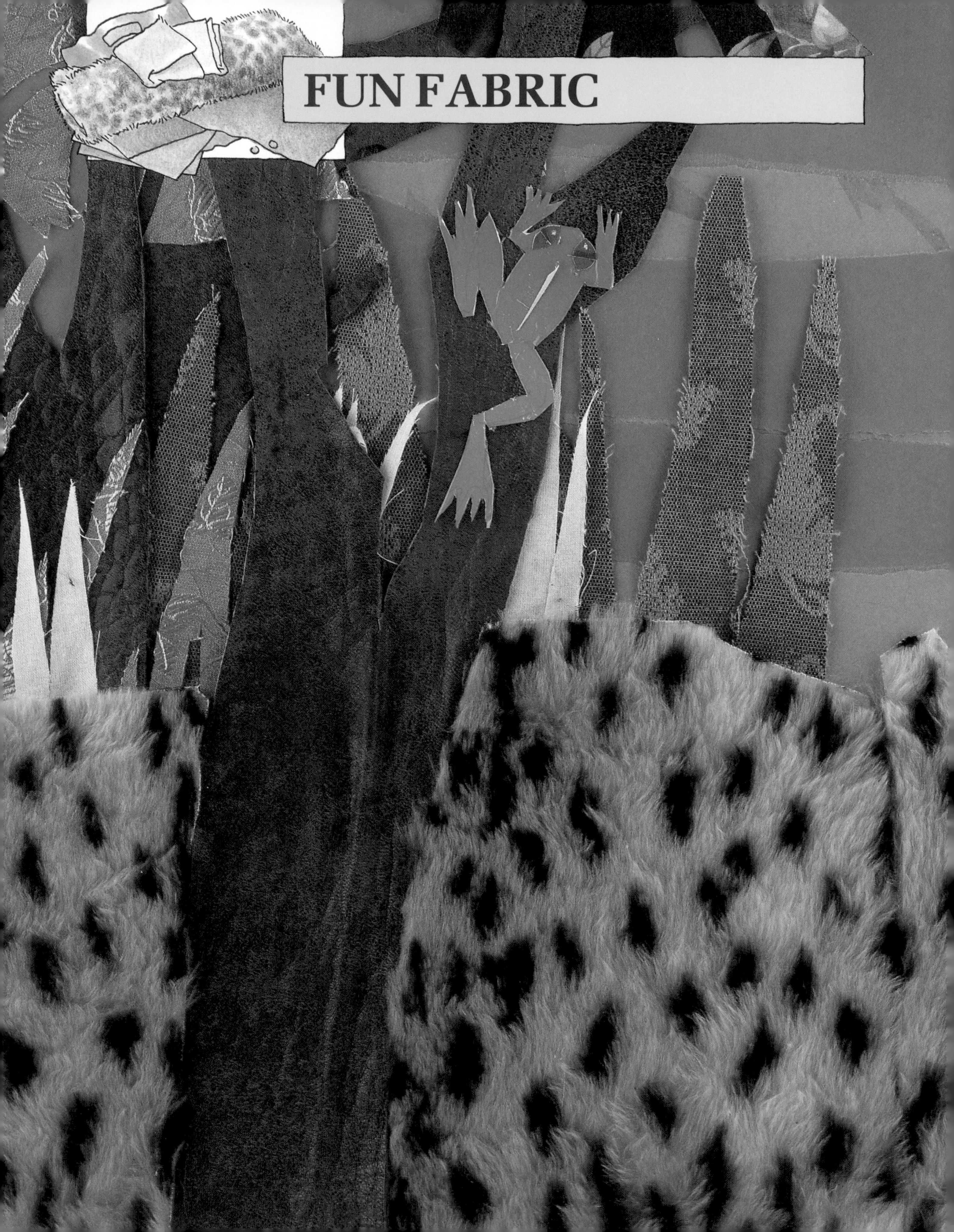

Fabric collages aren't just interesting to look at — they can be fascinating to touch, too. Collect scraps of material, and see what they suggest to you — velvet is soft and luxurious, plastic is smooth, silk is shiny, burlap is rough and coarse. Add more texture with yarn, ribbon, lace, and net.

1

Sketch a design for your collage, and collect your material. To make this jungle scene, we used fur fabric, leather, curtain samples, scrap paper, and a plastic bag.

2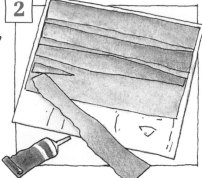

Always start with the background. To make a sunset sky, tear orange paper into strips and paste over blue paper.

3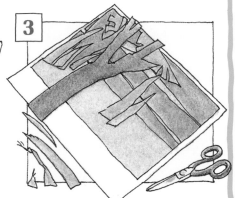

Cut and paste the jungle in place. The trees in front are wider than those at the back to make them look closer.

4

The leopard is made from fur fabric, while the frog is made from a green plastic shopping bag! Use more scraps to make the features — sequins are good for highlighting the eyes.

FOOD SHAPES

Dried pasta, beans, lentils, loose tea, and eggshells — many types of dried food can be used in collage. This frog is stuck together with glue in the usual way — but you can also make collages that are good enough to eat! Try making a delicious "collage" on crackers using diced ham, cheese, and tomato — or press candy into the icing on a cake!

Draw a frog on cardboard, and cut it out. Collect some dried beans, split peas, lentils, and loose tea.

Use a pencil to divide the frog's body into different areas of color. Cover some of these areas with glue.

Take a handful of beans or lentils, and press some of them onto the areas you have covered in glue.

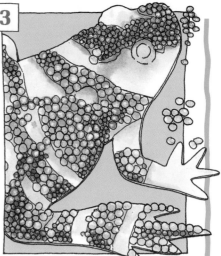

Contrast the bright orange lentils with the green peas. Use the loose tea to make the black stripes on the frog's body. For an eye, you could glue on a circle of black paper.

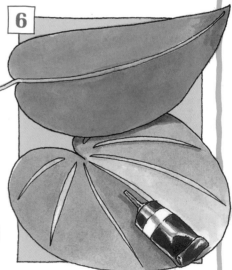

Use tinfoil to add a glimmer to the eye. You can highlight the frog's "scales" with a little silver paint. Finally, for a shiny wet-look frog, add a coat of varnish.

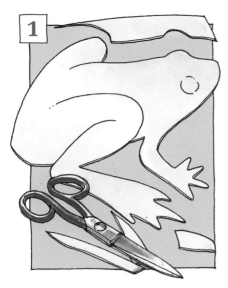

Give your frog a leaf to sit on. This can simply be cut from green cardboard or paper, or made from scraps of green fabric.

1

Cut a piece of card-
board, the same size
as one side of the box.
Glue on a sloping floor.

2

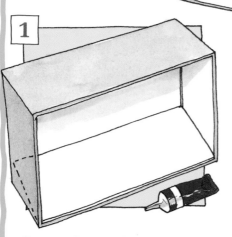

Glue torn colored
tissue paper inside
the box to make a
background scene.

Don't leave beach souvenirs to molder on the windowsill — turn them into a 3-D collage! You'll need shells, pebbles, and sand, plus a cardboard box, tissue paper, and thin cardboard. Old toys with a beach theme can complete the scene.

3

Cut a sand castle from Styrofoam or thick cardboard. Cut circles to make rocks.

4

Glue the rocks and castle to the floor. Paint the rocks. Glue shells to the scene.

5 Brush the floor and castle with glue and sprinkle on sand. Cut out palm tree trunks and leaves from paper.

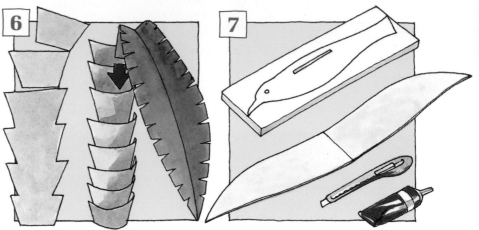

6 Cut the trunks into segments. Glue each one separately to the back of the box, and tuck in the leaves.

7 Draw gulls' bodies and wings on white cardboard. Cut a slot in the middle of the bodies for the wings, and hang the gulls from the top of the box with thread. Finally, see if you can find some old toys or decorations to add to your scene.

Left: 3-D collages are a great way of displaying your favorite models!

WALL FLOWERS

Once flowers, ferns, and leaves have been thoroughly dried or pressed, they should keep forever. Use them simply to make pictures or cards — or combine them with fake flowers to make a window box bursting with color, like the one overleaf. Never pick wild flowers — they could be very rare.

1

2

3

Pressed Flowers

Press petals, leaves, or ferns in a flower press, or between the pages of a heavy book. Leave them to dry for about a month. The flowers can then be glued into a picture with white glue.

Tissue Flowers

1. Make a simple template from cardboard. Use it to cut about ten flowers from tissue paper — use more than one color if you like.

2. Staple the flowers together in the center.

3. Fold up each petal in turn, as shown.

Window box

This midsummer window box can be made to bloom even in the depths of winter — all you need is some colorful paper and cardboard. If you like, you can include pressed flowers and leaves, or silk roses like the ones shown in the picture.

1

Cut a window frame from cardboard or paper. Cut a second frame, with slightly thinner bars, and glue it over the first one.

2 Cut a window box from brown paper. Cut out some "S" shapes, and glue the tips to the window box as shown.

3 Glue all your fake or real flowers to the window box. Fill in the gaps with extra leaves cut from colored cardboard.

JUNK MIRROR

Everything from screws and bolts to straws and string can be used in this project. You can also add toys, or figures modeled from clay.

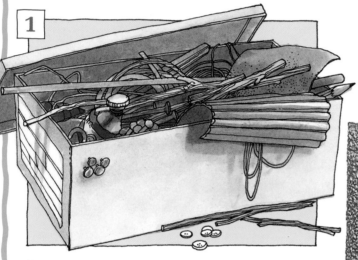

1

Gather up some junk, glue, a small mirror, and corrugated cardboard.

2

Cut two bases, each the same size. Cut a hole from one base for the mirror, and glue the two bases together.

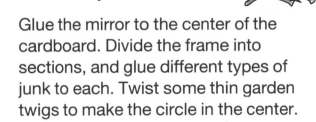

3

Glue the mirror to the center of the cardboard. Divide the frame into sections, and glue different types of junk to each. Twist some thin garden twigs to make the circle in the center.

4

Paint the mirror frame, and seal it with a coat of varnish. Ask an adult to help you attach a picture hook to the back to hang the mirror up.

CRASH!

If an alien intergalactic space cruiser from the year 3000 were to crash unexpectedly through your bedroom wall, it could look something like this...

1

Make a large cone from thin cardboard. Trim the bottom of the cone to make the shape shown.

2

Cut thick cardboard into a starburst. Paint it black, and glue or tape to the cone when dry.

3

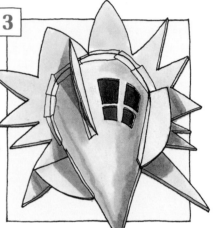

Cut window holes in the cone. Cut fins from cardboard, and glue to the top of the cone.

4

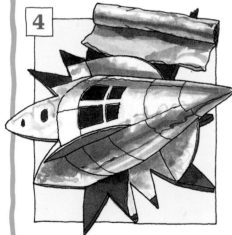

Cover the cone and part of the star with foil, so that it looks like a spaceship crashing through a hole.

5

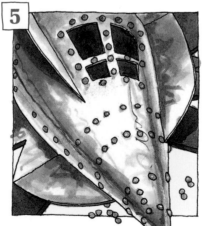

Glue split peas or lentils to the spaceship to look like rivets. Brush the rivets with silver paint.

6

The little star ship commander was made from pipe cleaners, beads, and colored paper!

EGGOSAURUS

The last dinosaurs died out about 65 million years ago. Some had razor-sharp teeth. Others had weird-looking crests or knobbly horns. But only the terrifying *Eggosaurus* was made from packing material, egg cartons, and plastic bubblewrap...

1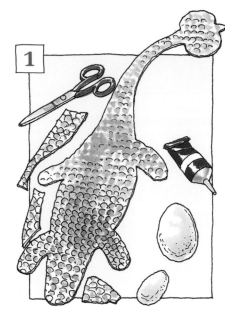

Draw an outline for the *Eggosaurus* on cardboard, and cut it out. Use it to cut the same shape from bubblewrap, and glue this to the cardboard.

2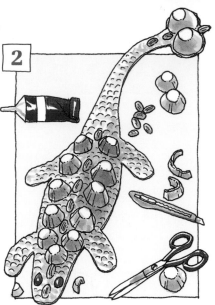

Cut up an egg carton, and glue the cups to the body. You can add extra scaly texture with dried peas or beans, seeds, bottle tops, shells, or net.

3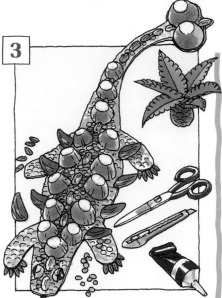

Color the *Eggosaurus* with thick poster paint. Cut some red ribbon or paper into a tongue, and glue to the mouth.

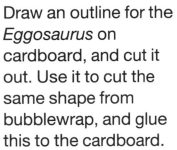

Stand the Eggosaurus *among trees with modeling-clay trunks and leaves made from green paper.*

MEMORY BOARD

Vacations, birthdays, or a special day out can all be recorded forever in a collage. All you need to do is to save any scraps or souvenirs and glue them onto a board made from cardboard, cork, or Styrofoam. Hang the board on your wall — every time you look at it, the happy memories will start flooding back!

1

For a Christmas souvenir, cut a piece of thick cardboard into a Christmas tree shape. Paint one side green.

2

Arrange the souvenirs on the board. When you like the way they look together, glue, pin, or staple them in place.

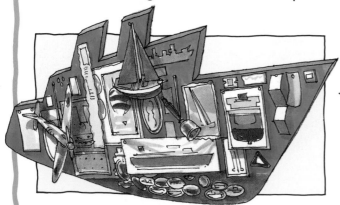

From a dream vacation to a walk in the park, you can use your souvenirs to make a 3-D bulletin board...

COLLAGE CARDS

Homemade cards are a million times nicer than anything you can buy in a store — ask any mom or dad! A selection of collage ideas from the previous pages of this book was used to make the cards shown below. In addition to looking wonderful, they're all incredibly quick and easy to do.

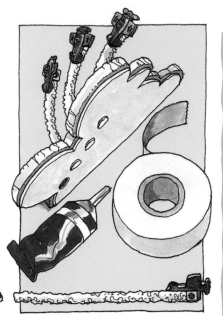

Cut or tear paper into strips, and paste them to make a simple land-scape. Use fur fabric or cotton to make the sheep in the foreground.

A hole punch can be a very useful tool in collage. How else could you make a hundred snowflakes in under a minute?

Four airplane-shaped buttons, white pipe cleaners, and a cloud cut from white Styrofoam were used to make this card.

MORE IDEAS

By now, you have probably realized that anything that stays still long enough can be turned into a collage. Here are a few ideas you may not have thought of...

Make strange-looking people or animals by cutting up different photos, postcards, or pictures and gluing them together. This is called photomontage...

Paste photos or pictures onto lampshades, wastepaper baskets, boxes, etc. Or glue dried pasta, candy, or cookies to jar lids. Finish them with a coat of varnish...

Collect everything you can about a friend's favorite subject (a sport, movie star, hobby, etc.) and make a collage as a special present.